Turkey Soup

for the *rest of us*

Peter Taylor

Doubleday Canada

Canadian Cataloguing in Publication Data

Taylor, Peter
     Turkey soup for the rest of us

ISBN 0-385-25897-6

1. Canadian wit and humor (English).*   I. Title.

PS8539.A93T87 1999   C818'.5402   C99-931183-2
PR9199.3.R365T87 1999

Cover and text design by Stray Toaster
Text illustrations by Martin Lender
Printed and bound in Canada

Published in Canada by
Doubleday Canada, a division of
Random House of Canada Limited
105 Bond Street
Toronto, Ontario
M5B 1Y3

WEB 10 9 8 7 6 5 4 3 2 1

Turkey Soup

for the *rest of us*

The author humbly dedicates this little book to the people who cry when they whack their funny-bone against a steel framed door, then howl with laughter when the same thing happens to someone else.

Introduction

Venimus, cecidimus, cecidimus in nostras nates.
(We came, we saw, we fell on our asses.)

The president of the United States gets caught with his pants down. The future king of England dreams about being a common tampon. The prime minister of Canada defends his family against a midnight prowler with a soapstone carving of a loon.

Turkey Soup for the Rest of Us is a heartfelt tribute to the dedicated men and women who came to our planet years ago to do dumb stuff — and thereby make the rest of us look good.

Where they came from, we don't know, but rest assured, they're everywhere, and they're here to stay.

So here's to the guy in Edmonton, Alberta, who forgot to pull on his balaclava until he was halfway through a bank robbery, and to the little lady in Muncie, Indiana, who attempted to blast a stubborn callus off her foot with a shotgun.

Here's to the six hundred people who paid $10,000 each to an Italian travel agent promising flights to Mars, and to the otherwise normal peeping Tom who hid in the tank of a women's outdoor toilet in a public park.

Originally, if you follow the news, there were probably fewer than a dozen of these happy, dedicated souls.

They'd crop up on the evening radio or television news, the announcer invariably signalling their arrival with the phrase, "And now for something completely different."

They showed up on the front pages of newspapers, in stories neatly boxed to warn the reader that the content, while straining the boundaries of common sense, was true.

Like jokes, these stories travelled fast and well — from barstool to barstool at the end of the day, and around the world on newswires, e-mail, and the Internet.

We read them to each other over the telephone, or clipped and stuffed them into envelopes with letters to friends and family at home or away.

And then, of course — as we say today — the stories, and the people in them, moved uptown.

Overnight, there were too many stories to brighten up the front pages of newspapers, so they spread through papers from front to back, even producing, along the way, such syndicated columns as Chuck Shepherd's "News of the Weird", the infamous "Darwin Awards" and several copycat versions on the Internet.

There were too many to simply tag on to newscasts, so entire radio and television shows were born, *America's Dumbest Criminals* being but one.

Suddenly, or so it seemed, the world went postal, and everybody wanted in on the act.

Behold the world of John Wayne Bobbitt, Marv Albert, Pee-wee Herman, Tanya Harding, and Dolly the Sheep.

Suddenly two doctors announced they'd found a way to lengthen my penis. But wouldn't you know it, one of them is a Dr. Long — and the other is (get this) a Dr. Stubbs. (Who to choose? Who to choose?)

But wait, there's more.

The Mounties sell their marketing rights to the Disney Corporation, the Reverend Jerry Falwell tells me Tinky Winky (my favourite Teletubby) is probably gay, and (I'm not making this up!) an eighteen-year-old Stettler, Alberta guy eats his underwear, hoping the cotton will absorb the alcohol before he takes a breathalizer test.

Has the world gone mad? Is it a cry for help?

We laugh at the guy who falls on his ass when he slips on a banana peel, or at the pompous twit who gets hit in the face with a well-tossed cream-filled pie.

We laugh at the clown who steps on the tines of a garden rake and is soundly smacked between the eyes.

It's a nervous laughter, say the people who take the time to analyse these things; not cruel, we're told, perhaps perverse; most likely, simply a way of saying, "I sure am glad that wasn't me."

But you gotta laugh, and I hope you *do* laugh at the stories and the people in this book.

Acknowledgements

The stories retold in this collection are all true, in that they have all appeared — in one form or another — in newspapers, or made their way into television and radio newscasts. Many were sent to me by friends from the newspapers that originally published them or came to Canadian newspapers via the various newswires who gleaned them from those papers to spread to other papers around the world. Still others came by way of long-distance telephone calls in the middle of the night, or as clippings shoved into Christmas and birthday cards. For the most part, the stories were chosen for the almost punch-line quality that destined them to be plucked like jokes from their original sources and then spread, barstool to barstool around the world.

U.S., Canada ease restrictions on free flow of stupidity between nations

EDMONTON, Alberta — When George Paquette is picked up for robbing a corner store in downtown Edmonton, police admit they had a better-than-ordinary description to assist them in their fairly speedy arrest.

The nervous forty-year-old, it turns out, was well into his robbery routine when he remembered that he'd plumb forgotten to haul his balaclava over his face.

MODESTO, California — And, not to be outdone on the other side of the border, twenty-two-year-old Richard King is red-faced when he's caught red-handed while doing his best to pull a quick armed robbery without a gun.

The old hand-in-the-trenchcoat pocket trick just doesn't cut it when the high-strung lad pulls his hand from his pocket and starts waving a pointed finger and cocked thumb menacingly at a grinning teller on the other side of the counter.

You can hide, Al,
but you can't cook

CARRIZOZO, New Mexico — When Canadian fugitive Allan Charles Whitequill finds a place to hide for the night, he can't believe his luck.

Right there for the taking are a room for the night, a microwave oven, and — a frozen turkey.

Talk about having died and gone to heaven!

Talk about maybe wishing you had!

According to arresting officers, the Regina, Saskatchewan, fugitive from justice appears to have badly misjudged the timing on the microwave and undercooked the turkey.

It was while dining on that rare bird, police speculate, that the ravenous Canadian was hit with what they politely describe as the *New* Mexican version of an old Mexican malady, and accidently locked himself in a bathroom.

By the time police finally came to his rescue the next morning, this galloping gourmet had punched a hole through the washroom wall in a vain and desperate attempt to free himself from one very smelly latrine.

No word yet from the turkey

MADISON, Wisconsin — Madison's police chief, Richard Williams, pops a bit of leftover turkey into the microwave and retires to his living room to watch TV while the meal heats up.

Within minutes, the chief dives for cover as the sounds of gunfire echo through his home.

Chief Williams later admits that the microwave is just one of the clever hiding places he uses to store his service revolver against the possibility of it being discovered by an intruder.

As a lesson to other members of the force, Williams gives himself a one-day suspension without pay for violating policy on the safe storage of firearms.

Peek-a-poo, we see you

PETERBOROUGH, Ontario — A very embarrassed twenty-six-year-old from Richmond Hill, Ontario, appears in court, charged with hiding in the holding tank of a ladies' outdoor toilet in a nearby park.

He was charged when two young women reported being more than just a little bit shocked by someone sneaking a peek at them, up through the toilet seat of the outdoor john. According to a police spokesperson, this fellow had lowered himself through the toilet seat and into the "bowels" of the campground latrine.

Police say the odoriferous offender, reeking to high heaven of excrement, was arrested near the scene.

Amid much snickering, chuckling, and an occasional guffaw, the accused tells the judge he doesn't have a lawyer and asks for a day or two to line up legal aid.

"I'm terribly sorry, would you mind calling back after dinner?"

WINNIPEG, Manitoba — Here's a cautionary tale for people who like to make life hard for telephone solicitors.

Les Newman, an artist who once worked as a telephone marketing researcher, opens a show at a Winnipeg art gallery in which he features the phone numbers of people who were rude to him.

"It's an opportunity for petty revenge," he admits, though he adds that only those people who "went out of their way to be particularly mean" are included in his work.

Not a cauliflower ear?

NAIROBI, Kenya — After a doctor successfully removed a bean that had become lodged in their daughter's ear, a Kenyan couple claims the doctor stuck it right back in when they told him they couldn't afford his fee.

Local newspapers report that after completing the procedure, the physician handed the smiling parents a bill for 350 shillings (approximately $8.25).

The parents told the doctor they had exactly 265 shillings, and were attempting to arrange credit when this master of bedside manners reinserted the offending bean.

The Kenyan Medical Association is now investigating.

Now that takes balls!

VICTORIA, British Columbia — Fired from his first gig after a rambunctious seven-year-old yanked off his beard and kicked him in the groin, a shopping mall Santa is canned again for fondling his privates on TV.

The not-so-jolly St. Nick says he wasn't fondling himself — he was simply showing a curious acquaintance where he's been kicked by the little monster at the other mall.

Not good enough, says the merchants' association, adding that they aren't in the business of upsetting customers, and that too many parents caught the offending crotch-grab on TV.

It sorta loses something in the translation

WELLAND, Ontario — Store owners across Canada receive a warning from head office to be on the lookout for a singing Santa doll when a customer complains that the one he bought is crooning "Rudolph the Red-nosed Dickhead" and several other spiced-up versions of Christmas classics.

Despite the store's offer of a full refund, Charles Zarb says he'll keep the $22.95, battery-powered doll that his wife bought him for his birthday.

Zarb, who collects Santas, says it's the only one he has "that talks like this."

A spokesperson for the chain of stores explains that the novelty Santa dolls are manufactured in China.

One man's gibberish . . .

BRANTFORD, Ontario — A doll is sent packing back to where it came from when a Brantford family hears it "teaching" their two-and-a-half-year-old daughter to swear.

The "Berry Luvin' Baby Smurf" is supposed to speak twelve different phrases when you squeeze its hand, says the manufacturer.

But according to the little girl's parents, the foul-mouthed doll has a one-track mind. "Who gives a fuck?", is all it will say.

The store where the toddler's grandmother purchased the doll as a Christmas present removes the last six "Baby Smurfs" for testing.

Three of the six seem well-versed in the twelve expressions they are supposed to utter. The others, says a company spokesman, speak only "gibberish."

You wouldn't treat me like this if I was a man

KITCHENER, Ontario — A knife-wielding bandit grabs a bouquet of flowers and leaves in a huff when the stubborn attendant at a local gas bar refuses to turn over cash or cigarettes.

Police are looking for a slim young man in a cream-coloured dress with plunging V-neck and black trim.

Accessories, investigators say, include a brown- and pumpkin-coloured jacket, a pink and green scarf, and white running shoes.

In addition to the posies, police say the bandit snatched a package of sausages from a display before fleeing the store.

Also called to the scene were the fashion police.

Elementary, dear Watson, he simply 'tuque' the money and ran

OTTAWA, Ontario — He reeked of alcohol and was wearing a tuque, an Ottawa florist tells officers investigating the daytime robbery of a neighbourhood flower shop.

At a nearby bar, police arrest a tipsy forty-two-year-old who fits the description to a T — as in tuque — and find his pockets stuffed with wads of cash.

And there, mixed in with the wads of cash, is a hold-up note.

I'll take the history of flight for $500, Alex

TORONTO, Ontario — Faced with the irate father of a Toronto teenager or an opportunity to leap buck-naked from a fifth-storey balcony into the bushes below, the teen's twenty-two-year-old lover opts for the latter, breaking his hip and leg in the early morning fall.

Still, he's one lucky fellow, according to police.

Had he landed on the concrete pathway instead of in the hedges surrounding the apartment building, he probably would have been killed, they say.

They decline to comment on what might have happened if the fellow had opted to stay on the balcony. According to police, the young lady's father showed up unexpectedly and discovered the naked young man in his daughter's bedroom.

Stuck on you . . .

NAIROBI, Kenya — It was hardly the stuff of Harlequin romances when an amorous police constable and the wife of a village elder found themselves "locked in a passionate embrace."

Sources say it took doctors to separate them, and police used tear gas to break up the hordes of villagers who came for a glimpse of this close encounter of a decidedly different kind.

Dispatches from Reuters claim the adulterous duo panicked when they became stuck, and dialled for an ambulance. It was then, reported the *Kenya Times*, that all hell broke loose.

According to witnesses, the town ground to a halt as dozens of curious locals stopped what they were doing and made their way to the hospital to witness the tangled affair.

Bring on the tear gas.

When police finally managed to disperse the mob, the couple was flown to Nairobi where what God had curiously joined together, doctors managed to pluck asunder.

Do you think I'm sexy, do you want my body?

FREDERICTON, New Brunswick — Some guys have a way with women. Some guys don't.

Take the guy who is hauled off the Fredericton-to-Moncton bus by fellow travellers when, apparently dumbstruck by the beauty of his seatmate, he attempts to seduce her by whipping off all of his clothes.

Unimpressed by his wooing technique, his heavy breathing, or his equipment (or possibly all of the above) the little lady yells for help, and the libidinous lout is held by her rescuers until police arrive.

And for another $15,000 I'll drop my G-string

TAMPA, Florida — A thirty-eight-year-old bachelor claims he saw stars, suffered whiplash, and felt as though he had been hit in the head by two cement blocks.

No, it wasn't the best sex he had ever had in his life.

The somewhat embarrassed young man was attending a bachelor party in his honour when, "without warning or consent," a topless dancer allegedly knocked him all but senseless with her oversized breasts.

Hell of a party, some might say, but for this fellow, the full-frontal assault has triggered a $15,000 lawsuit against the Florida nightclub Diamond Dolls.

The young lady whose "cement blocks" caused the pain, suffering, and mental anguish, among other complaints, dances under the stage name Tawny Peaks.

Shouldn't you guys be over at the doughnut shop?

GRIMSBY, Ontario — Some nights you're lucky, some nights you're not.

Giving up his struggle to pry open the window of a van, a determined would-be car thief discovers that one of the front doors has been left unlocked.

Climbing into the drivers' seat, the thirty-six-year-old parking lot prowler suddenly realizes that his luck for the day is all used up.

For it's then he finds himself eyeball to eyeball with a couple of chaps who appear to have arrived ahead of him.

Shades of a tired knock-knock joke that ends, "Sir who?" And the answer comes back, "Surveillance."

The men in the back of the van are cops on a stake-out, investigating a rash of car thefts in the area.

I'd like to report two robberies and an accident

TORONTO, Ontario — It's the short arm of the law for a thirty-five-year-old Toronto man who commits two thefts in less than an hour, then caps it off by crashing a stolen car through the front doors of a midtown police station, where he's arrested on the spot.

The whole thing started at 5 a.m., when a Toronto transit employee reported the theft of boxes outside a subway newsstand.

Minutes later, the man stole a car in which he sped several blocks before squealing to a halt in the lobby of 53 Division.

In addition to the thefts and possession of stolen property — surprise! surprise! — the man is charged with driving while impaired.

And a man who hires a fool for a lawyer . . . ?

FRESNO, California — Imagine the embarrassment — not to mention the confusion — in a Fresno courtroom when a lawyer and his client appear before a magistrate both wearing handcuffs and bright orange, jail-issue jumpsuits.

Alphonse Woods is dressed the way he is because he has not yet posted bail after being charged with drug possession, trespass, and obstruction of justice.

Appearing with him, and for him, is his attorney, Frank Dornay, who apparently forgot to turn up for a drug test — a stipulation of his own probation — also related to drug charges.

But for that kind of money, you really got screwed

CHICAGO, Illinois — It's not the first time that the graduate of Northwestern University School of Law and former associate at a prestigious Chicago law firm is charged and convicted of prostitution.

Trial evidence shows that her going rate, as published in newspaper personal ads, is three times what the law firm billed for her services.

When the moon hits your eye like a big pizza pie . . .

MILAN, Italy — Police say more than six hundred Italians were duped out of a total of $6 million by a team of con men promising seats on the first tourist flight to Mars.

For $10,000 each, the naïve, would-be astronauts were promised camel caravans across the vast Martian deserts, expeditions along the red planet's mysterious canals, and the breathtaking beauty of Martian sunsets.

If Mars was not their cup of tea, the con men offered shorter trips and weekend packages to the moon.

Investigators say the smooth-talking shysters have disappeared to parts unknown.

She was not an intellectual, or even pretty, but when she strode into the room wearing size 12 shoes, he felt himself drawn to her

NEW YORK, New York — On the subject of libel suits brought by real people who find themselves too thinly disguised in works of fiction, one U.S. lawyer boasts a solution to at least half of the problem.

"For a fictional portrait to be actionable," Leon Friedman tells an Authors Guild panel, "it must be so accurate that a reader of the book would have no problem linking the two."

Writers can avoid the problem, Mr. Friedman continues, by following what many libel lawyers are now calling "the small penis rule."

Who's going to launch a libel suit in which he has to admit about the character with the small penis, "I'm sure that's me!"?

Caught red-handed

OTTAWA, Ontario — A man pleads guilty to one attempted bank hold-up, and one real hold-up at the very same branch less than two hours later.

On what appears to have been a dry run, thirty-eight-year-old Ronald Burke walked into a downtown bank, behaving so suspiciously that a teller refused to serve him.

Undaunted, and obviously determined to be treated with a bit more respect, the by-now-familiar would-be bandit returned, this time demanding cash.

And this time he got it, along with a canister of identifying red dye that exploded as he attempted his getaway.

The envelope please . . .

DURHAM, North Carolina — An alert bank teller is credited with foiling the plans of a bold but not-too-clever con artist.

Police allege Keisha Yvette Gregory took a cheque made out to the Tension Envelope company into the bank, flipped it over in front of the teller, and signed it with a flourish — Ms. Tension Envelope.

The unidentified Ms. I Wasn't Born Yesterday was commended by her bank manager for her quick thinking when she called security.

Hey, c'mon, it was snowing, and hailing, and sleeting, and raining . . .

WHITE PLAINS, New York — After eighteen years of making her appointed rounds, a forty-nine-year-old letter carrier is fired from her job for walking too slowly.

"With each step," her supervisor writes in his assessment of Martha C., "the heel of your leading foot did not pass the toe of your trailing foot by more than an inch." That pace, postal authorities say, adds approximately thirteen minutes to the section of the route along which she was clocked.

When last we heard, Martha was appealing to customers along her route to help her save her job.

He knows if you've been bad
or good . . .

LONDON, England — A British postman is given a one-year sentence for protecting his customers from the evils of artificial sin.

Michael Hales, the court was told, had developed keen, if not X-ray, eyes when it came to "goodies" of a certain kind.

So good was Hales at spotting the distinctive packaging used by certain manufacturers that the thirty-eight-year-old bachelor had amassed a personal collection of eight mailbags full of vibrators, condoms, dildos, pornographic magazines, and other sex toys addressed to customers along his routes.

What next? A ban on batteries?

HUNTSVILLE, Alabama — Until a federal judge threw cold water on it, the State of Alabama boasted one pretty stiff penalty for anyone caught selling vibrators — "a $10,000 fine and a year of hard labour," according to one of six Alabama ladies who challenged the year-old statute.

Conceived as a way of reining-in strip clubs, the new law made the selling of sex toys illegal as well.

The law's infringement on the privacy of the bedroom sparked the challenge that overturned the statute.

In shutting down strip clubs, one plaintiff complained prior to the federal ruling, the state was taking away public entertainment. In going after vibrators, she added, those spoilsports were now trying to take away a person's right to entertain herself.

The three stooges go to jail

TORONTO, Ontario — Three suspected kidnappers chase a man into a building in the heart of Toronto's Chinatown, totally unaware in the heat of pursuit that they have followed the fellow straight into the spacious lobby of the city's downtown 52 Division.

"I guess they didn't stop to read the address," says Detective Sergeant Stewart Wighton at a press briefing the next day.

Police allege the three suspects entered their chosen victim's home, claiming that he owed them money. Accepting the plea that the young man had no money but knew where to get some, the three forced him into the rear seat of their car and set out to pick up the cash.

At a nearby red light, the victim bolted, fleeing on foot. The three suspected kidnappers followed hot on his heels, and straight into the arms of the law.

Choreographer wanted

OSHAWA, Ontario — Curly, Larry, and Moe move over; when it comes to comedic choreography, there are three new kids on the block.

When a police van transporting prisoners to a downtown courthouse pulls into the parking lot at the rear of the court, three men in the rear of the van make a sudden break for freedom that witnesses describe as high burlesque.

Handcuffed together, and apparently running in all directions, the threesome manages a less-than-graceful fifty-metre dash until — BOING! BOING! BOINK! — they wrap themselves around a telephone pole and come to a dazed, head-banging halt.

Pursuing jail guards whisk them off to their next performance — a special appearance before a judge.

They should issue these guys with helmets

TORONTO, Ontario — When the suspect he is arresting becomes violent, Constable Marc Beausoleil calls for help and help comes running — unfortunately, from opposite directions.

Two responding officers run into each other with such force that one is taken to hospital with a concussion. The other slips on a patch of ice, injuring his leg.

Meanwhile, Constable Beausoleil is having trouble breathing, and collapses.

Justice has its day, however, when uninjured officers finally make the arrest.

30

I know you're in there . . . not!

OAKLAND, California — Police spend two hours, and fire a total of ten tear-gas canisters, in an attempt to smoke out an armed gunman who has barricaded himself inside a house in downtown Oakland.

During a lull in the negotiations, officers discover the suspect in their midst, shouting for the gunman to come out and surrender.

Spin, Spin, Spin

ROCHESTER, New York — Commenting on her guilty plea for driving while under the influence, New York assemblywoman Susan John opines, "This will give me additional insights into the problems of drinking and driving."

Ms. John, chair of the Assembly's Committee on Alcohol and Drug Abuse at the time of her arrest, says the experience will allow her to do her job "more effectively."

EXETER, Rhode Island — Meanwhile, John Bergantini, a local candidate for tax assessor, is sued for $2578 in back taxes.

Will this harm his chances for election? Mr. Bergantini thinks not, saying his ability to write a good cheque has absolutely nothing to do with his ability to judge how much a piece of property might be worth.

So, we'll call it 'Drunk Drivers Against Drunk Driving'

BRANDON, Manitoba — The founder of a university chapter of Students Against Drunk Driving is handed a fourteen-day jail sentence after pleading guilty to impaired driving. It's his second impaired driving offence in five years.

"When he's sober, he's very much against drunk driving," his lawyer tells the court.

Now that's what I call leadership

NEW YORK, New York — AT&T lures John Walter into its ranks with a $22-million incentive for quitting his previous job, then nine months later ousts him from his position as president and chief operating officer with a close-to-$4-million severance package.

The reason for his axing? He did not provide the "intellectual leadership" the company needed.

Writing in various trade journals, industry wags point out that the $26 million it cost the company to acquire and fire Walter translates to approximately $18,000 an hour for the nine months of his tenure.

At last report, the "intellectual leaders" who hired and fired him are still providing sage counsel to the telecommunications giant.

And over here, you got your Germany, and over here . . .

VANCOUVER, British Columbia — A British Columbia rancher arrives home convinced he's stepped into a hurtin' song — his house is gone, his barn is gone, his chicken coop and the fence around his cows are gone.

They've been blown to smithereens by his neighbours.

Greg Loring's neighbours — the Canadian army's Military Training Reserve — had launched an early morning raid on his thirty-hectare spread, deeming it "enemy territory" during war games in the Chilcotin area of the British Columbia interior.

Initially denying responsibility for the incident, Canada's Defence Department finally coughs up a $150,000 out-of-court settlement when the militia admits that the attack on Loring's property was the result of using the wrong map — one on which Loring's ranch appeared to be on the army's land.

Xena, Princess Warrior 44DD

OTTAWA, Ontario — In yet another breakout of military intelligence, Canada's National Defence Department unveils plans to produce a combat bra as part of a $184-million program to put the country's forty-two thousand men and women into form-fitting, fighting form.

A spokesperson for the Clothe the Soldier Program points out that while women's bras do come in an exotic array of designs, shapes, and sizes, none is entirely suitable for the violent, physical activity one might encounter in combat.

To the best of his knowledge, the spokesperson adds, Canada's will be the first army in the world to provide its troops with war bras.

Still more boobs as soldier fails to consider the ten percent who actually sign up

COPENHAGEN, Denmark — And in Denmark, Major O.P. Soerensen comes under fire from his own troops when, on the advice of a manufacturer, he orders identically sized bras for the more than five hundred fighting women of the Danish army. The manufacturer, according to Soerensen, claimed a C-cup, size 100, was perfect for ninety percent of Danish women.

Who's that raunchy little lady with all the medals?

VANCOUVER, British Columbia — Al Charters doesn't need Viagra. And he sure as hell isn't interested in a sex-change operation.

But according to the Second World War veteran, those would appear to be his options.

After months of trying to obtain a basic hearing aid from the Veterans' Affairs Department in Ottawa, Ontario, he reads that the government will be picking up the cost of Viagra for military personnel.

Next, he learns that the military, in special circumstances, has decided to pay for sex-change operations.

"Utterly ridiculous," he fumes.

Al Charters may be a little hard of hearing, but now, he says, he's heard it all.

"Emergency Police Response Headquarters, would you mind holding please?"

HAMPTON, Virginia — Ron Carter enters the Turkey Hall of Fame when he calls police to report a bomb at a bar down the street from the bar in which he is drinking.

Police say Carter figured that with so many squad cars speeding to investigate the bomb scare, he could make it home without any fear of being pulled over for impaired driving.

It takes the tipsy thirty-nine-year-old so long to report the impending doom that the dispatcher traces the call and officers walk in on Carter seconds after he hangs up the phone.

Bombs away!

TORONTO, Ontario — Transport Canada officials promise to investigate a piece of frozen excrement that crashed through the roof of Mr. and Mrs. Neseveremko's North York home.

"It was like an explosion," says Mr. Neseveremko.

He and his wife were watching television when the chunk of waste smashed through their ceiling and landed on the carpet.

Spokesmen for the police and fire departments say the material almost certainly was dropped from an overhead jet. However, public affairs manager Bruce Reid of Pearson International Airport insists that incidents of frozen waste being jettisoned from aircraft are extremely rare.

The case of the kamikaze cuckoo

WILLIAMSBURG, Virginia — Call it love in full flight, but there's the fabulous Fabio taking a whirl on a roller-coaster with a clutch of adoring, toga-clad ladies, when SPLAT! — he gets the bird!

Beak-to-beak, *mano-a-oiseaux*, the handsome hunk who adorns the covers of hundreds of hot-love, bodice-ripper novels is left dazed and spitting feathers when an errant bird flies into him, striking him right between his beautiful blue eyes.

There to launch a new ride — "Apollo's Chariot" — at Busch Gardens, the cover boy with the flowing hair is whisked off to hospital, treated for cuts and scratches, and released.

The bird, alas, will never read another book.

God 1, Josh Rempel 0

CALGARY, Alberta — A sixteen-year-old Calgary teenager is so exasperated by his mother's unflinching faith in religious matters, that he challenges God — if there is a God — to strike him with a bolt of lightning on the spot.

God may have been busy that day, but the following morning He zaps Josh Rempel good, burning a hole in his baseball cap and scorching his hair as the doubting Thomas runs under a tree to escape a thunderstorm.

The young man, now a believer, spends the day in the hospital.

And God said unto Dick, "It's time for your six-month checkup"

LETHBRIDGE, Alberta — Dentists, unlike God, it seems, do not work in particularly mysterious ways.

They do fillings, they pull teeth, they scrape away plaque and, for the right price, they'll decorate your smile with a flashy gold tooth.

So when Dr. Jack Sherman hears evangelist Dick Dewart claim that God has granted him a gold tooth in answer to his prayers, he gives Dewart a call to remind him that he, not God, gave Dick the gleamer some ten years back.

Dewart, the president of CJIL-TV, made his claim about the miracle molar during a Christian TV fund-raising telethon.

After the good doctor's telephone call, Dewart calls the whole thing an honest mistake. He says he remembers having a silver tooth, not a gold one, and thinks the change from silver to gold has been heaven-sent.

And for my next trick, I'm going to attempt to paint my toenails while bungee jumping

MUNCIE, Indiana — A woman who used a shotgun in an attempt to blow a callus off her foot after a bout of heavy drinking is taken to the hospital for psychiatric evaluation.

The thirty-eight-year-old is reported to be in good condition the day after discharging the .410 shotgun in her backyard.

According to police, the lady claimed she had polished off a "gallon of vodka and two or three beer" before trying to blast the offending callus from her foot. She told officers she already had attempted to cut away the callus with a razor, and was afraid the damned thing was getting infected because it hurt so bad.

They shoot Oldsmobiles too, don't they?

SPRING HILL, Tennessee — They sure do things differently in the South.

When his '88 Oldsmobile died on him, did Boyd Kelly pound the dashboard, kick the tires, and curse his luck while hiking down the highway towards a pay phone to call the nearest auto club?

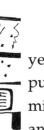

No siree, bub.

The thirty-nine-year-old simply pulled out his AK-47 military assault rifle and pumped ninety rounds into the stalled car right there at the side of the road.

Police say motorists reported the bizarre incident after coming upon the all-out, armed attack as they drove along the highway.

Kelly, who told police he just lost it when the car conked out on him, is charged with a weapons offence, then freed on bail.

You sure that wasn't
Raymond O'Cruz?

SCHERERVILLE, Indiana — A .40-calibre pistol and a blood-alcohol reading of 0.18 percent are a tricky mix at the best of times.

Throw them together on St. Patrick's Day, and stand back.

Police report that Raymond A. Cruz was celebrating with friends at a bar when he became so upset with a slow-flushing toilet that he pulled out his handgun and shot it full of holes.

Cruz was arrested at the scene and charged with weapons offences and resisting arrest.

According to arresting officers, no other patrons of the popular nightspot were in the washroom at the time.

Please, this is a hold-up, thank you

BIRMINGHAM, Alabama — Claiming to have a gun, two very polite and obviously well-bred teenagers are arrested for the attempted robbery of a shoe store after a clerk asks them if they would mind waiting for the demanded cash because she is very busy with another customer.

They comply, and are still waiting patiently, and politely, when police arrive in response to a silent alarm.

Now you may boldly go where no man has gone before

HONG KONG — Face-lifts, breast enhancement, tummy tucks, and liposuction are but a few of the tricks some women try when it comes to creating the perfect package for the perfect mate.

But looks alone, at least in China, may not be enough.

There, according to a Hong Kong wire service, young women are flocking to Ghangshou province, where for as little as U.S.$500 they can revisit virginity at a hymen restoration clinic.

Not wanting Mr. Right to know about a Mr. Wrong or two, the bride-to-be travels to the clinic for the procedure once her suitor has popped the question and the date for the wedding has been picked.

Next they'll be asking for the "after" shots . . .

TORONTO, Ontario — A twenty-three-year-old woman is not amused when a government employee requests a photograph of her breasts.

The strange request came as a result of the woman's decision to have a breast reduction operation, and was made after her doctor had submitted the necessary approval forms to the government's claims office.

A government spokesman explains that the "before" photos only show the applicant from the neck down, and are seen only by medical consultants.

But Dr. John Toye says he can't believe that anyone can assess the need for an operation simply by looking at pictures.

The lady agrees: There's no way she's baring her breasts, especially for the government.

You can't hide, Sammy, so you'd better learn to run

NEW YORK, New York — Sammy "The Bull" Gravano severs family ties when he turns state's evidence and helps put crime boss John Gotti behind bars for life.

Sammy further estranges himself by helping author Peter Maas with *Underboss*, a biography of Sammy that further exposes the workings of the mob.

Sammy's reward from the state, of course, is automatic membership in the federal Witness Protection Program — plus a brand-new face, thanks to extensive plastic surgery.

So sure is he that his new look will attract ladies into his life, the recently divorced Sammy allows Maas to use a current photo of him in the book.

I'm in the mooooood for love

STOCKHOLM, Sweden — And if ever there was a candidate for the witness protection program, our vote goes to the fifty-year-old man from the Gothenburg region of western Sweden who admits in court to having had sex with two cows — not once, but twice.

A veterinarian, testifying at the trial, says the cows probably did not enjoy it, and suffered physically and emotionally from the experience.

The midnight cowboy says he was watching pornographic films when he became aroused and headed for a neighbour's farm armed with his vibrator and a video camera.

Two weeks later, he was back again.

The guy was reported to police, and charged with cruelty to animals, when he brought the film of his romp in the hay to a photo lab for developing.

Don't mess with Max

JOHANNESBURG, South Africa — Isaac Mofokeng learns the hard way — always look before you leap.

The twenty-five-year-old robbery suspect is running from police when he leaps over a wall at the Johannesburg Zoo into the not-so-warm embrace of Max, a 120-kilogram lowland gorilla.

Poor Isaac.

In the resulting mêlée, the gorilla rips off his jeans, bites him on the buttocks, grabs him by the right leg, swings him around like a limp rag doll, and hurls him against a wall. Police drop Max with a tranquillizer dart, and rush the dazed suspect to the hospital.

"I thought my time had come," the suspect tells a Johannesburg court while pleading not guilty to charges of burglary and robbery.

Next time, wear the farm dog outfit

BLAIRSTOWN, New Jersey — It's a Halloween to remember for a thirty-four-year-old local woman and her two daughters when they are attacked by a fox as they commence their evening of trick-or-treating.

The woman says the possibly rabid animal suddenly appeared out of nowhere when her four-year-old daughter climbed out of the car to call at a neighbour's door.

Police say the youngster was dressed up as a rabbit.

Waiter, there's a mule in my soup

BEIJING, China — Chinese officials blame restaurant rivalry for an outbreak of food poisoning when close to 150 diners become gravely ill after dining on one restaurant's specialty — donkey soup.

The soup, according to news reports, was poisoned by the owner of another restaurant when he became upset by the brisk business enjoyed by his competitor.

SWF with body cast, cuts, scrapes, and abrasions seeks companion

MOSCOW, Russia — If you ever run into Olga Karpov in downtown Moscow, you can always treat her to dinner in a hospital cafeteria.

According to a Russian news agency, Olga is single, readily available, and — no thanks to her slightly unorthodox method of meeting guys — still quite lively.

Police say the man-hungry young Muscovite was arrested after causing at least eight accidents by jumping in front of cars driven by handsome young men. She told police she hoped the men might ask her out, to make up for knocking her down.

Each of the accidents sent her to hospital, but no dates resulted.

I know this sounds crazy, but haven't we met somewhere before?

AKUREYRI, Iceland — In northern Iceland, police say, it's possible to drive all day and never see another car.

How then to explain the bozo who rams into the same woman driver twice in the same day?

The first time he slams into her, he's exiting a parking lot.

Less than twenty-four hours later, he nails her again — this time as she's driving a rented car through a downtown intersection.

Before she met up with the one-man demolition derby, the lady tells police, she had an unblemished record of twenty years without an accident.

French fries, anyone?

ELMSDALE, Prince Edward Island — Five motorists in Prince Edward Island cause a fire that destroys a potato-packing plant by using a cigarette lighter to help locate their gas tank.

The group had run out of gas and were pouring fuel into the vehicle from a portable container when the vapour ignited. In the ensuing panic, they heaved the burning gas can into a stack of wooden crates, which in turn ignited the building causing $1 million damage.

No ifs, ands, or butts

CHARLOTTE, North Carolina — A local cigar aficionado insures a box of rare cigars against fire, enjoys them at his leisure, then files a claim with his insurance company for the loss of the lot in a series of small fires.

The company balks, claiming the man's "small fires" were nothing more than the matches he struck to light the cigars.

In a unique ruling, a judge cites the insurance company for not clearly spelling out what kind of fires the company would consider uninsurable, and awards the man $15,000 for the loss of his precious stogies.

The victory, however, is short-lived, when — as soon as the fellow cashes his cheque — the insurance company has him arrested on twenty-four counts of arson. This time a judge finds him guilty, and sentences him to one year in jail.

Oh, no! Not Winnipeg!

GIMLI, Manitoba — The defence rests, Your Honour.

A thirty-four-year-old Gimli woman, charged with arson, says she got so fed up with furnace and heating problems that she burned her house to the ground.

"I didn't do it for the money," Dawn Harrison tells the court. "I hated that house. I just wanted out."

Her lawyer argues that his client was suffering from serious financial and domestic problems at the time of the incident. He reminds the court that she hasn't even claimed insurance on the $90,000 home.

Finally, he tells the judge, his client is so embarrassed by what she has done that she has moved to Winnipeg.

The judge, who may or may not have ever been to Winnipeg, lets her off with a one-year conditional sentence.

"I'm wearing a blue serge suit with a silver badge, and shiny black boots . . ."

VIENNA, Austria — In the throes of lust, or possibly stupidity, a thirty-two-year-old Austrian actually gives his phone number to a woman who says she's just too busy for heavy breathing right now, but will call him back when she's free.

Police say the obsessive caller admits to placing as many as thirty-thousand obscene phone calls over the previous couple of years, including close to 180 to the "busy" lady over a six-month period.

Dial 'M' for Mumsy

LONDON, England — Two red-faced lovers have some explaining to do when, in the throes of passion, one of them accidentally hits the speed-dial button on a bedside phone and twice wakes the young lady's mother in the middle of the night.

The first time the phone rings, the woman in Devizes, southern England, assumes that the grunting and groaning on the other end of the line is the misplaced passion of an obscene phone caller, and goes back to sleep.

On the second call, amid even more moaning, Mom hears a man's voice in the background and, unmistakably, the sound of her daughter.

Her daughter was screaming, "Oh my God!" the woman tells police, when she frantically dials 999, the emergency response squad, to report a break-in, a mugging, or even worse.

Police say the young couple was quite embarrassed when the emergency team burst into the apartment, and grew even more embarrassed while explaining the freak accident.

Now, of course, they have some explaining to do — to Mom.

A good stiff drink

COPENHAGEN, Denmark — Call it one last bid for quality time, but residents in Copenhagen are still scratching their heads at the antics of Flemming Petersen, who decided to have a final outing with his dear old (departed) dad before the funeral.

Two days after his eighty-six-year-old father had passed away, Petersen sneaked the body out of the morgue, decked the old fellow out in motorcycle leathers, and roared off down the highway for one last ride.

Along the way, reports say, Petersen pulled into a roadside bar where he propped the deceased up in a booth and, according to the bartender, seemed to be having a good old father-son chat for the better part of an hour.

Flemming Petersen was fined $470 for the day's outing.

Gone, but not forgotten

BROCKVILLE, Ontario — A twenty-nine-year-old Brockville man sues his dead mother, claiming that while she was still alive she fell on him and broke his ankle.

His mother fell on him when she tripped while getting out of her chair to dance with him, he tells the judge, who awards the man $13,000 from his mother's estate.

Whether the ruling will encourage other young men to dance with their mothers on a regular basis remains to be seen.

She looked too natural

COPENHAGEN, Denmark — Relatives at the funeral of an elderly family member call the whole thing off when someone notices that the woman in the coffin doesn't look familiar.

A spokesman for the funeral parlour discovers that the family's loved one was interred two days earlier in a ceremony attended by another grieving family that hadn't noticed the difference.

Hospital officials blame human error, saying that when two elderly ladies died, their bodies were sent to the same funeral parlour with improper identification.

The mix-up is corrected when the funeral parlour disinters the first body for reburial, and buries the second woman free of charge.

This is *living*?

LONDON, Ontario — While saying that such mistakes are rare, a spokesman for the province's health insurance plan admits that someone in his department informed an eighty-one-year-old London area woman that she was dead.

Not only was she dead, she was told, but if she persisted in using her health card, she would be charged with fraud.

OAKVILLE, Ontario — In a similar bureaucratic blunder, a seventy-nine-year-old Oakville man shows up on a list of the no longer living and the government cancels his federal pension.

Asked by the man's son just how his father is expected to survive without his monthly pension, a government spokesperson says he can always apply for welfare.

And at 60 clicks, the fridge door pops open

NEW YORK, New York — Ask any thirteen-year-old: It's people like David Allison who give adults a bad name.

Allison, an obesity researcher with St. Luke's–Roosevelt Hospital, is the inventor of the "TVcycle," a Rube Goldberg contraption guaranteed to draw the scorn of couch potatoes and junk-food addicts alike.

Hooked electrically to the television set, the stationary bicycle allows TV watchers to view their favourite shows only when they pedal.

Tests, says Allison, show that the bicycle has already helped youngsters lose weight *and* has reduced the number of hours they spend in front of the set.

Yes, it is quite beautiful, but I've totally forgotten where I got it

TORONTO, Ontario — A thirty-three-year-old Toronto man with a taste for fine art and fine dining mixes the two with disastrous results. He's sentenced to ten months in jail after the former neighbours he invites to dinner are surprised to see several *objets d'art* that were stolen from their own home two years ago.

The couple informs the police, who say that a subsequent search of the young man's home turned up not only the couple's antique prayer rug and valuable Chinese platter, but more than $100,000 worth of paintings lifted from the University of Toronto's Trinity College.

Also discovered on the absent-minded fellow's premises — a $5000 Ming dynasty figure that had gone missing from the Royal Ontario Museum, where the man had previously worked as a gardener.

C'mon, do you know what a cab costs from here to my place?

TORONTO, Ontario — What do Torontonians do when the court finds them guilty and takes away their driving licences?

A surprising number walk out of the courthouse, climb back into their cars, and drive away, according to police.

Police make the discovery while monitoring a parking lot outside a courthouse and are amazed when as many as eight people who had pleaded guilty to, or been found guilty of, traffic offences simply climb behind the wheel.

The eight people are arrested again — and charged again.

Yet another damned out-of-work actor/bank robber

CALGARY, Alberta — A spectacular car chase and head-on collision ends up on the cutting room floor when two bad actors are arrested on a movie set and carted off to jail.

Turns out the two have just robbed a bank and are fleeing from police when they swing their getaway car onto a residential street being used in the production of the Hollywood film *Snow Day*.

Witnesses say many people were initially confused: was this real, or was it in the script?

The brief encounter with the wonderful world of make-believe ends, however, when the getaway car smashes into a police van that has also driven onto the set.

The men are arrested, police find the loot from the heist in the trunk of the car, and it's back to make-believe for everyone else.

Cut!

The short-sleeved arm of the law

TORONTO, Ontario — In an inspired attempt to deter speeders, Toronto traffic cops install a series of plywood traffic officers along several residential streets in the city's west end.

The idea, according to a police spokesperson, is that speeding drivers will ease up on the gas pedal when they spot the life-sized cut-outs standing on the shoulder of the road.

In a letter to the *Toronto Star*, a sharp-eyed motorist says he wasn't fooled for a minute. The cardboard cops are wearing short-sleeved summer shirts in the middle of November — brrrr!

If only his parents had bought him that tricycle

WINDSOR, Ontario — A thirteen-year-old student steals his teacher's $50,000 Saab 900SE Turbo convertible for a joyride and is arrested when he rolls into a nearby service station asking for an oil change.

The day before he is to appear in court for sentencing on the Saab theft, the teenager is stopped at a police roadblock north of Montreal, behind the wheel of a stolen Cadillac.

Someone's been sleeping in my bed . . . and here he is

KINGSTON, Ontario — A Kingston area woman who hasn't called a taxi is surprised to find one parked in her driveway when she arrives home, and is even more surprised when she finds the driver, freshly showered, exhausted, and asleep, in her bed.

Rudely awakened, the drowsy, disoriented guest bolts from her home. Police arrive to find a stolen cab in the driveway, as well as a wallet stuffed with ID conveniently left on the lady's bedside table.

Police say the forty-year-old burglar had been out of jail for barely two days when they quickly tracked him down and returned him to more familiar surroundings.

Why people down east don't lock their doors

PORT HAWKESBURY, Nova Scotia — Thieves break into a shop in this Nova Scotia town and steal a diamond ring. Which in itself would not be remarkable except for the fact that one of them brings it back to the same shop the next day to have it appraised.

Prosecutors are expected to urge that the two thieves serve out their sentence in a local aquarium, under glass.

Of all the coppers in all the towns in all the world . . .

OSHAWA, Ontario — When the suspect he was questioning pulled out his driver's licence, Constable Andy Hickerson knew he had his man.

The licence was Hickerson's own — lost in downtown Oshawa, along with his wallet, several weeks earlier.

A further search of the suspect's wallet also turned up one of the constable's credit cards.

While admitting that police work is often ninety percent luck, one officer says the chance of a culprit using a policeman's own licence as identification has to be millions to one.

Mother always said I shouldn't hitchhike

NASHVILLE, Tennessee — Quenton Hughes is so grateful to the driver who picks him up hitchhiking that he offers him a small bag of crack cocaine.

The driver declines and instead drives Hughes directly to jail.

It turns out Hughes has been picked up by Detective Derry Baltimore in his unmarked police car. It also turns out that Hughes was wanted for shooting a woman during an armed robbery outside a local nightclub.

Dumber and dumber

BELLEVILLE, Ontario — A Belleville man breathes a sigh of relief when the judge hands him a one-day sentence for a drug charge, then gasps at his own stupidity when, turning out his pockets before heading to the prison cells, he produces a bag of marijuana.

The prison official gasps too, and marches the nineteen-year-old back into the same courtroom, where he's charged with possession for the purpose of trafficking and breach of probation.

MEMPHIS, Tennessee — Meanwhile, south of the border, eighteen-year-old Brandon Hughes goes to court to fight a routine traffic charge.

As he raises his hand to swear his oath on the witness stand a gram of cocaine falls out of his sleeve and onto the courthouse floor.

He too is charged with possession — on the spot.

Blowin' in the wind

SASKATOON, Saskatoon — In a case of clearly being in the wrong place at the wrong time, Francois Blanchette of Edam, Saskatchewan, pleads guilty to possession of marijuana.

The forty-eight-year-old organic farmer and amateur artist had set up his easel to dab a little paint, and smoke a little joint on a quiet corner of the campus at the University of Saskatchewan.

Sadly, the breeze blew his smoke directly through the window of a nearby classroom, where a group of police officers happened to be attending a training course.

Blanchette is assessed a fine of $300.

 **Next . . .**

TOPEKA, Kansas — Responding to a telephone call from a suspicious customer, police storm a downtown "Kwik Shop" and find the cashier tied up at the rear of the store and the greedy, would-be robber serving customers from behind the counter.

The store clerk tells investigating officers that the thief originally asked for all of the money in the cash drawer. Angry and disappointed at the small size of the take, the man tied up the clerk and went to work.

Oops!

LOS ANGELES, California — Police in Los Angeles still chuckle over the impulsive robbery suspect in a precinct line-up.

Each man in the line-up was asked to step forward and shout the words, "Give me all of your money, or I'll shoot."

Caught up in the drama of the moment, the impulsive suspect took several steps towards the two-way glass and suddenly blurted, "That's not what I said."

We're mad as hell and we're not going to take it anymore

APPLETON, Wisconsin — A woman successfully sues her psychotherapist for $2.5 million, but won't be splitting it with anyone.

In her suit, the woman claimed that her former doctor was treating her for multiple personality disorder. She said he had convinced her that she was harbouring over one hundred personalities — including those of Satan and a duck — and was billing her insurance company for "group therapy."

Now I know why they call it a dumb waiter . . .

HAMILTON, Ontario — Two university students on a "pantry raid" spend the night between floors when the dumb waiter they are using to sneak into a restaurant beneath their apartment grinds to a stubborn halt.

After a claustrophobic night in the elevator shaft, their cries for help are finally heard by kitchen staff arriving for the morning shift.

Police say rescue workers, assuming they were freeing one person from the elevator shaft, were amazed to discover two people in the tiny, cramped elevator box.

"They were awfully happy to see us," a rescuer comments as police charge the two students with theft.

A bus trip to Timmins gets you a 'C'

TORONTO, Ontario — A part-time instructor at Toronto's Centennial College is bounced off the campus when police lay charges in a marks-for-money scam after students complain.

The thirty-six-year-old math instructor promised students an A+ in return for money or airline tickets.

According to investigators, the instructor hounded students who were doing badly in his courses, promising top grades in exchange for the cash and tickets.

The students, it seems, preferred to earn their marks the old-fashioned way, and refused the offer.

From Sir with love

HASTINGS, Minnesota — A former science teacher is placed on six months' probation for helping four high school students etch tattoos into their skin with nitric acid.

The boys, aged fifteen and sixteen, had asked forty-year old James Bartholow for assistance with the procedure. Although Bartholow tried the nitric acid on his own hands first, when applied to the students' arms it caused third degree burns resulting in permanent scarring.

Bartholow pleads guilty to charges of child endangement and agrees to pay a fine of $900, plus the boys' medical expenses.

That's my story, and I'm stickin' to it

TOKYO, Japan — A Japanese university professor ends up in court after stripping off his clothes in a karaoke bar and riding one of his female students like a pony.

Asked to explain himself, the randy professor says he was attempting to imitate an early equestrian statue.

"It was art," he tells the judge.

The judge may not know much about art, but he knows what he likes, and he doesn't like this.

The professor is fined $2800.

Sticking his toes in other people's business

TORONTO, Ontario — A retired schoolteacher who installed a video camera in his shoe so he could film up women's dresses is ordered to perform 150 hours of community service after he pleads guilty to mischief. Judge Ted Ormston also gives the man an eighteen-month probationary sentence.

Calling the sixty-three-year-old a "peeping Tom of the 20th century," Crown counsel informs the court that a custom lens in the toe of the man's shoe was linked to a waist-pack camera by a special wire that ran up the man's trouser leg.

According to police, at the time of his arrest, the man had videotaped under the skirts of as many as fifty women. Over two days during the Canadian National Exhibition alone, say police, he taped close to two hours of film. Police say the man would slide his foot between the feet of unsuspecting young women while they were playing "midway games." The women were so intent on the games that they didn't notice the stranger behind them.

When the women leaned over to toss a ring, throw a ball, or to shoot in a shooting gallery, the man would activate his camera.

Do as I say, not as I do

DAVIS, California — A bookstore employee makes a citizen's arrest and calls the police when a University of California–Davis professor is accused of shoplifting.

Investigating officers say the professor allegedly walked out of the campus bookstore with a $20 textbook without paying.

Refusing to comment on the event, a university spokesman says only that the professor teaches courses in criminology, juvenile delinquency, social deviance, and law at the Davis campus school.

Jail's too good for them; a year in the south of France, I say

TORONTO, Ontario — A Toronto man is charged with mischief when police find a miniature camera hidden in a tanning parlour, and several dozen videotapes of naked women in the man's home.

With no idea when the camera was installed or who the women caught on film might be, police ask any women who have ever used the tanning salon to come forward.

An investigating officer says there is nothing to suggest that "electronic peeping" is a widespread problem.

He may be right.

Charged with a similar offence, a Kingston area man pleads guilty to doing the same damned thing, but in a more traditional way. Using a mirror on the end of a stick you can get a pretty good peek at the woman in the tanning booth next to yours, that fellow explains.

Next time, go with forget-me-nots

VERONA, Italy — A man whose fiancée broke off their engagement gambles that sending one rose for each day of the four years he and his fiancée were engaged might win her back.

Response: an indifferent "thanks, but no thanks" from the woman, and a $9,000 bill from the florist.

No, who's on first; what's on second

DETROIT, Michigan — Darryl Fletcher is in love, so when his sweetheart gives birth to a bouncing baby boy, he's elated.

Brandon Ventimeglia is also in love, so when his sweetheart gives birth to a bouncing baby boy, he's elated too.

What neither man knows is that they are dating the same woman.

For two years after the birth, India Scott manages to orchestrate the men's visits to see their son.

The men finally meet when Scott announces that she is in love, and leaving Detroit to marry another man.

Fletcher sues for custody of his son.

Ventimeglia sues for custody of his son.

The two agree to blood tests to settle the question of which man is the real dad.

Neither is, as it turns out, and Scott leaves town.

Your government cares about you

SMITH FALLS, Ontario — After four years of chasing her ex-husband with the help of the province's child support offices, a thirty-eight-year-old mother discovers that the man she had written off as a deadbeat dad has been making his payments all along, like clockwork.

It turns out the provincial office handling his child support deposits has been sending them to a woman down the road — another single mother with the same name, living on the same highway, with the same postal code, and also expecting child support payments from an ex-husband of her own.

Government officers say more than $7000 went to the wrong woman, and that the mother who received the money by mistake, who has four children of her own to support, should pay it back.

'Til death do us part

DUBLIN, Ireland — A month before laws permitting divorce are enacted by the courts, an elderly Irishman wins a "divorce in advance," claiming he is so ill that he might not live to be free of his loveless marriage.

The gentleman remarries within days of the court granting his wish, then dies three days after the wedding.

They just kept saying they had headaches

ARLINGTON, Virginia — It took twenty-four-year-old Margaret Hunter four months to discover that the man who said "I do" on her wedding day not only wouldn't, but couldn't.

Hunter is awarded $265,000 in her lawsuit after finding out that her twenty-six-year-old hubby is in fact a woman, Holly Anne Groves.

SANTA ANA, California — It takes Correen Zahnzinger four years to discover that the man of her dreams is not what he seems.

She also sues, after three years of courtship and one year of marriage, when she uncovers the fact that Mr. Right is really Ms. Wrong — a twenty-nine-year-old trickster named Valerie Inga.

Tear down the house and put up a parking lot

TORONTO, Ontario — Driving a front-end loader and armed with the jealous rage of ten jilted lovers, a thirty-three-year-old Toronto man rips the front off a house and demolishes four cars.

Police say this fellow has been brooding since he discovered that the object of his obsession is planning her wedding to another man.

According to neighbours, the love-struck lad used the bucket of the front-end loader to toss two cars out of the driveway before attacking the house, and destroyed two others while ripping down the garage in which they were parked.

Sadly, one of the cars — a flashy, new Corvette — belongs to his dearly beloved's new fiancé.

A picture's worth a thousand words

EDMONTON, Alberta — Sometimes it's better to stick with flowers, or maybe a nice card from the wonderful folks at Hallmark.

An Edmonton man is given a twelve-month suspended sentence after sending a photograph of his genitals to a magazine. The gentleman insists he was only trying to find a girlfriend, and thought the photo was on its way to an adult magazine.

As luck would have it, his Kodak moment ended up in the mailbox of a Calgary businesswoman.

The judge is unmoved, and convicts him on charges of mailing obscene materials.

Damned joggers, they're everywhere

TORONTO, Ontario — A twenty-seven-year-old exhibitionist escapes "double exposure" when a judge reverses an earlier ruling that would have required the man to appear in public wearing a sign on which were printed the dirty details of his deed.

The man, charged with masturbating in front of joggers, had been found guilty and sentenced to spend five mornings a week in downtown Toronto wearing a sign that read: "I've been convicted of committing an indecent act in High Park."

Appealing the ruling, the accused's lawyer argued that such unusual punishment would expose her client to ridicule and the possibility of vigilante justice.

In overturning the previous sentence, the appeal court asked that the man seek psychiatric counselling and stay away from city parks for the next eighteen months.

Dog gone, but love is still blind

SYDNEY, Australia — Police say an eighty-one-year-old blind woman hired thugs to steal a seeing-eye dog from a fifty-year-old sightless lady when she learned that her former husband was having an affair with the younger woman.

Investigators say Phyllis Gration, who runs the Lady Nell Seeing Eye Dog School, was devasted when she learned of the affair, and demanded the return of the dog, which had been obtained from her.

Marlene Massingham refused, and the feud continued until several months later, when Massingham was shoved to the street and the dog was kidnapped while they were out for a stroll.

Two men, say witnesses, crammed the dog into a car and drove off.

Greg Cooper, the man at the centre of the dispute, met Ms. Massingham while working at his wife's school, and moved in with her following his divorce from Gration.

Cooper is forty-seven.

Officers should be on the lookout for a funny little guy with a goofy moustache

NIAGARA FALLS, Ontario — Hitler's gone!

One minute he was there, standing between Bugsy Siegel and Timothy McVeigh, and the next, he was gone.

Officials at the the Criminals Hall of Fame Museum believe the thieves walked out of the tourist attraction arm in arm with the life-sized, wax figure of the Nazi madman.

Hitler was a little man, a staffer explains. He'd be very easy to tote.

Oh yeah, first you case the joint

SEATTLE, Washington — Given one more chance to try his hand at armed robbery, David Zaback undoubtedly would avoid a gun shop.

Ignoring the fact that the shop just might be jammed with card-carrying, pistol-toting, NRA sharpshooters, the thirty-three-year-old Seattle native commences his hold-up routine by firing several shots into the air as he approaches the cashier.

In the eerie silence following the burst of gunfire, the would-be robber hears nothing but the sound of clicking as well-armed staff and customers unholster and cock their guns.

No one knows how many rounds are fired, but Zaback is hit at least seven times, and dies several hours later in hospital.

Hey, you shoulda seen the other guy

NEWARK, New Jersey — A twenty-seven-year-old Bergen County man is rushed to the hospital after shooting himself in the arm and leg with his own gun while pistol-whipping another man during a fight.

Andre Gordon, charged with assault, illegal possession of a firearm, and various drug offenses, is treated for gunshot wounds and released from hospital.

Police say his .380-calibre handgun fired while he was using it to club his victim on the street.

The victim, twenty-five-year-old William Jones, receives treatment for facial scratches and lacerations.

And for my next trick . . .

HAMILTON, Ontario — In what his girlfriend describes as a "drunken accident from hell," a thirty-three-year-old Hamilton man tries to swallow a friend's metre-long sword.

Witnesses say he had managed to swallow about thirty centimetres before things went tragically wrong.

The man is rushed to the hospital, where he is treated for a collapsed lung, a cut throat, and damage to his voice-box.

It was a dumb stunt, according to his girlfriend.

"I mean, I love him with all my heart," she says, "but what a jerk."

Sometimes a red card doesn't cut it

JOHANNESBURG, South Africa — In what is thought to be a first in South African soccer, a referee has killed a player.

The incident took place when a player lunged at the official with a knife, protesting a goal. The referee shot him.

The Invincible Empire strikes back

BALTIMORE, Maryland — Things are going swimmingly for a Maryland county's Adopt-A-Road program until a chapter of the Ku Klux Klan applies to sponsor a stretch of highway. According to the program, local civic organizations are rewarded for picking up litter with a sign that acknowledges their participation — which would mean a billboard reading, "This highway was adopted by the Invincible Empire Realm of Maryland."

The Klan's application is rejected.

But when the KKK challenges the county with the help of the American Civil Liberties Union, arguing that the decision violates the Klan's right to free speech, the county decides to scrap the whole program.

Come fly with me . . .

ST. ANDREWS, Manitoba — A man finds an airplane with the keys in the ignition, climbs in, taxis down the runway, and takes off into the wild blue yonder.

A simple case of airplane theft?

Not quite, according to local authorities, who say that while the impulsive thirty-two-year-old apparently may know a thing or two about flying, he doesn't know how to land.

Two hours after take-off, the man makes several abortive attempts to land the Piper Cherokee before heading off to Winnipeg, where he finally crashes.

Airport spokespersons say the single-engine plane's tires blew out on impact, and the propeller dug into the runway as the plane came to a halt.

Police caught up with the would-be pilot as he fled the crash site on a bicycle he had loaded into the stolen aircraft.

Go, magic fingers . . .

WINNIPEG, Manitoba — A twenty-one-year-old bakery worker gets the mother of all head massages when he's mauled by an amorous dough kneader while inspecting the interior  of the machine.

Co-workers aren't sure why, but say the unidentified young man stuck his head inside the industrial-strength bakery equipment and accidentally started it up.

The thumping, pummelling, buffeting, squeezing experience sends the fellow to the hospital where, feeling more than a bit like the Pillsbury Doughboy, he's examined by doctors.

He may have forgotten to look both ways but he *was* wearing clean underwear

FORT LAUDERDALE, Florida — Who doesn't remember, as a kid, putting coins on the railroad track to flatten them?

So, maybe it's a guy thing.

Kevin Sean Rowe remembers, and tries it again with disastrous results.

Reliving a boyhood memory, the thirty-year-old journalist places his quarter on a southbound track, and then stands back to let the approaching train flatten it.

In the noise and excitement of that little bit of recaptured youth, what Rowe fails to notice is the northbound train that flattens him.

Rowe, a writer with the alternative weekly *New Times*, ends up with a fractured skull, a dislocated shoulder, several broken ribs, and a collapsed lung.

"There's not many people as stupid as yours truly," Mr. Rowe tells a fellow journalist. "I should be dead."

His neurosurgeon, Don Krieff, doesn't disagree, saying he can't imagine anything stupider than an educated, normal guy out playing with a train. "Luckily," he adds, "he should be fine."

Unarmed, but dangerous

PARIS, France — A twenty-one-year-old Frenchman, knocked off his motorcycle in a hit-and-run accident, picks himself up, dusts himself off, and starts off home again — without his arm.

Doctors say post-traumatic shock may explain how Olivier Faure was able to walk and hitchhike the ten kilometres to his home without noticing that his left arm had been ripped off at the elbow.

According to police, the young man's mother noticed her son's arm was missing when she helped him off with his coat.

Fast-acting medics were able to find the arm at the scene of the collision and rush it — and Faure — to the hospital, where the arm was successfully reattached.

Sleeping through the National Dream

OSHAWA, Ontario — An Oshawa man who took a nap on a railway track was not even aware he'd been run over by a train.

Spotting a person in the middle of the tracks, the engineer pulled the emergency brake but was unable to stop the locomotive. Emergency crews, police, and firemen were quick to arrive, expecting a corpse, but were amazed to discover the man sleeping quietly, unhurt, and unaware.

The man, whose name has not been released, had apparently staggered out of a nearby bar and passed out between the rails. "If he'd woken and sat up," observed a police spokesman, "he would have been in serious trouble."

Now, let's hear you cough with a Welsh accent

TORONTO, Ontario — A man charged with attempted murder is set free when a jury foreman coughs before delivering a guilty verdict and the judge interprets the cough as a "not."

The thirty-two-year-old is half-way across the courthouse parking lot when a juror asks the judge why the man is walking away.

CARDIFF, Wales — Meanwhile, on the other side of the ocean, a judge sentences an innocent man to two years in prison when a juror's cough drowns out the "not" in "not guilty."

The confused man is set free when a juror asks the judge why the poor fellow is being carted off to jail.

A nearly clean getaway

TRENTON, Ontario — Friedle Lempay is asleep in the car when her husband pulls off Highway 401 at a service station to use the rest room.

Waking up, she decides to visit the ladies' room herself. When she returns, the car has vanished. Her husband, refreshed but unobservant, drives for an hour along the highway before police catch up with him to let him know that his wife is waiting for him back at the service centre.